Self-Acceptance

The Secret to Happiness

By: Stan Kozak

For more great books on topics like this please check out my author page on amazon:

http://www.amazon.com/Stan-Kozak/e/B016SMX0RI

Table of Contents

Legal Warning

Chapter 1

Introduction

The road to self-acceptance can be long and winding, with many stumbling blocks. The truth is that we, ourselves, place most of the stumbling blocks in the way. The well-known, saying, "I am my own worst enemy" is particularly true on this journey. Have you found yourself living in a constant state of worry? Are you anxious about deadlines and competition at work? Do you worry about whether you are doing the right things? Are you constantly comparing yourself, your children, your home or your car to other people or their possessions? Do you feel pressured to live a certain lifestyle? Have events like birthdays, vacations and holidays become more of a burden than a time of relaxation or celebration? If the answers to these questions sound familiar, then a lack of self-acceptance may have resulted in your living a lifestyle filled with anxiety.

Chapter 2

Building a Positive Self-Image

During the late 1960s, mental health professionals began to focus on the importance of building self-esteem in children. The premise was that many emotional well-being issues stemmed from a lack of self-esteem and that increasing self-esteem, thereby making people feel better about themselves, would solve these problems. Though there is nothing wrong with having a healthy measure of self-esteem, we now know that increased self-esteem, alone, is not the solution it was once thought to be. Many health professionals now advocate self-acceptance as the key to a healthy self-image.

Building self-esteem, alone, is ineffective because it is conditional and based upon approval. If you like yourself because you achieve something or are approved by others, then the converse may be true. Disliking yourself then becomes the norm when you feel you have failed or you feel that others are negatively judging you. Naturally, we prefer to be successful and do whatever we can to achieve it, even if we are trying to achieve an unreachable standard.

There is absolutely nothing wrong with striving for success. In, fact, it is very normal and healthy. It becomes unhealthy, however, when we set our standards too high or we base our standards on the approval of others. When these arbitrary standards are not met, we internalize the negative beliefs about ourselves and attach them to events throughout our lives. Self-esteem waxes and wanes based on success and approval from outside sources, therefore, constant anxiety may exist because even when you succeed, you may fail the next time! Human beings are imperfect and failures are going to come, so basing emotional well-being on self-esteem is a losing game. Since we all are imperfect, the key to well-being and happiness is self-acceptance and a positive self-concept. Self-acceptance can help reduce anxiety and self-defeating emotions and behaviors. Western culture, however, demands success and approval. How do you embrace self-acceptance when society is focused on the opposite?

A good place to start is with being honest with yourself, learning about yourself and the changes that are needed. First, you must come to the recognition that you are the one in control of how you feel and how you react to external circumstances. Yes, what is currently happening or what has happened in the past plays a role, but you are the one that creates your feelings. No event or person can MAKE you feel a certain way or do certain things. Coming to this knowledge can be an "a-ha" moment for many, but it takes more than an intellectual acknowledgement to achieve self-acceptance. It takes hard work, practice and consistency to change what may be life-long patterns. Old ways of thinking and behaving must be replaced with healthier models. This takes time and you may even find that you experience a relapse.

A problem lies in the fact that you cannot accept someone whom you do not know. Furthermore, if you do not have an accurate picture of yourself, or self-knowledge, then you have a more difficult time with self-acceptance. Building a healthy view of yourself starts with an honest self-analysis. Self-knowledge has its basis in childhood. Parents play an extremely important role in helping their children to know themselves. It is important to notice and learn about your child's likes, dislikes, feels, fears, wants, and needs. At a very young age, they learn about themselves through how you react to them. They will perceive their strengths and faults through you. It is so very important to help your child develop an objective and realistic view of themselves, devoid of judgments about their self-worth. Unfortunately, if a parent is too busy, depressed, abusing substances, or negligent, a child will not develop this vital self-knowledge. Whether the parent is ill-intentioned or not, the result is the same – an adult who does not know himself, cannot properly accept himself and has diminished happiness.

You may not have the self-knowledge that you need to achieve optimal happiness. In fact, the various techniques that aid self-acceptance that are described in this book all involve a measure of self-analysis or self-reflection. A good self-analysis begins with an understanding that you have an internal self-critic – a "voice in your head". First, you must come to terms with the fact that your internal critic is serving some purpose in your life. It may be that your internal critic is a sort of a barrier that you have built to keep you from feeling pain or disappointment. You may even believe that you need this inner critic to keep you on the right track. The problem is that every time you listen to this critic, you are making it stronger. As the critic becomes stronger, so does your dislike for yourself and eventually, though you thought it protected you, your inner critic takes over and destroys every ounce of positive self-esteem in you. Recognizing your inner critic and its work, however, can be difficult. Much of its work is done without you being consciously aware. When something goes wrong in your life, your inner critic says, "I told you so!" and you accept the blame for whatever went wrong. When things are going well you would think that your inner critic would be happy. Yet, it is still at work, telling you that you just got lucky or it was some sort of accident. Many people who live in this vicious cycle classify themselves as overachievers or perfectionists and believe that these thoughts and criticisms are necessary to help them achieve their goals. Your inner critic is not very nice and does not play fairly either. It loves to compare you to others and uses impossibly high standards, always comparing you to the best. It also tells lies like: "you never do anything right", "you always mess up", "everyone hates you" etc.

The inner critic keeps a running tab of all your mistakes and failures and reminds you of them at the worst possible moment. It likes to call you horrible names like idiot, stupid, fat, worthless, failure. Living with an abusive inner critic can cause damage in so many ways and you may not even recognize it. The negative self-image that results from such abuse can cause you to underachieve or overachieve, both out of a fear of failure. It can cause you to constantly need to prove you are "good enough" and can make you hostile and offensive towards others so that they won't reject you before you can reject them.

Now that you are aware of the inner critic and the damage it can cause, you must go a step further to recognize when the critic is at work and how to control it. For a week or so, write down every negative though that you have about yourself and what purpose you think that those feelings serve. For example, "That person will never want to be your friend" may serve as a barrier to keep you from being disappointed. Then try to determine what benefit you get from these negative thoughts. If your inner critic is correct, what is it that you cannot accomplish? From what is your inner critic trying to protect you? Does the self-criticism push you to try to accomplish a goal? How could things be different if you did not have such thoughts and feelings? Journaling should provide valuable insight that can be used to stop the damage caused by your inner critic.

Next, you must practice thinking rationally and objectively about each negative feeling generated by the critic. If you can identify the purpose behind a negative thought and objectively assess it, then you can counter it with a healthier thought or feeling. Practicing this over and over will ultimately remove the inner critic's power and retrain your mind. There are a number of ways to accomplish this. When a negative thought enters your mind, you can simply tell it "Go away", "You aren't telling the truth" or "Stop". Once you have stopped the negative thought, you have to replace it with something positive, like "I am a good person" or "I am a worthy person". Finally, you must fulfill whatever purpose the inner critic was serving with a healthy method to achieve the same purpose. Going through this sequence removes any need for the critic.

Once you have quieted your inner-critic, you should spend some time examining all the good things about yourself. This will help you focus less on any mistakes or failures that occur. Mental health professionals often suggest that you make a list of your strengths and weaknesses in several different areas: appearance, relationships, personality, morals, work (school), art, sports, daily tasks, mental functioning, and sex. Next, underline all the negative characteristics and re-write them so that they are accurate criticisms and not over-exaggerations like the inner-critic typically uses. Do not make any negative judgments about yourself in the statements. You may only make statements about the behavior, not your value or worth. Also avoid drawing any conclusions about whether or not you are able to achieve a certain goal.

"Grant me the serenity to accept the things I cannot change, the courage to change the things I can, and the wisdom to know the difference." This prayer, commonly known as the Serenity Prayer, focuses, in part, on accepting the things that cannot be changed. Now that you have an accurate list of any weaknesses or faults that you think you may have, you must move a step further to understand

and accept them. First, reassess to make sure that they really exist. Make sure that you are not exaggerating. Think about whether other people think you have this fault. Are you placing too much emphasis on the alleged weakness? Can you compensate for the fault or correct it? Was the trait developed as a coping or survival mechanism for a problem that no longer exists? Once you have reassessed things, you have some choices to make: (1) you can change things that can be changed, (2) you can change how you feel or your reaction to unchangeable circumstances, or (3) you learn to accept things that cannot be changed, you choose to release them or you decide that they simply are not that important anymore.

Most of us have been told by our parents at one time or another that we need an attitude adjustment! In this case, it is true. Having someone tell you to have a good attitude is rarely the answer. How do you get rid of bad attitudes and replace them with good ones? Learning about the three components of every attitude is helpful as you try to modify your own. These are: (1) the cognitive or knowledge part (what you know, think, or believe about the person or situation), (2) the feeling or evaluative part (what emotions you have towards the person or situation), and (3) the behavioral part (your actions with the person or in the situation). Typically, the emotional part of our attitude is much stronger than the cognitive, more rational part, and has much more control over our behavior. We can cognitively know something to be the truth, but out emotions overwhelm us in a situation and override our ability to be rational. When trying to change a bad attitude to a good one, any of the three different components can be adjusted to change the others. For example, if you change your cognition, your emotions, thoughts and feelings should change. Likewise, changing your behavior can often change the feeling and cognitive part of your attitude. Finally, changing the strong emotions you have about something will, of course, change your behavior and your cognition.

As with our examination of the inner-critic, the first step in developing good, healthy attitudes is to openly and honestly assess your attitudes. You can do this through self-observation. Certainly there are things that you know about yourself. You can look outward to others and determine what they observe about your attitudes. Our behaviors are typically very well aligned with our attitudes. A self-exploration exercise can help you identify and learn more about your attitudes. Journaling your responses to these types of questions is very helpful. What kind of feelings do I have about a particular person, place, thing or situation? How strong are those feelings? Do these feelings need to be changed for any reason? Can they be changed? Are my feelings rational? Am I being overly judgmental? How did I develop these feelings? Am I using stereotypes or overgeneralizations? Am I basing my feelings off of what I think other people believe? Are there other perspectives that I need to understand? How are these feelings affecting my behavior? Do I want to change my behavior? Can I change the behavior directly or do I need to change my thinking or feelings first?

After this period of exploration, you will next delve into developing new attitudes. Different types of attitudes are advocated for from a wide variety of different sources. Self-help gurus define the types of attitudes that they feel are beneficial. World religions are filled with the different types of attitudes you should maintain. The employment industry has developed theories about the types of attitudes that will help you in the workplace. There are many attitudes that can help you cope with life's more difficult situations and self-acceptance is one of them. This book will delve into some common areas in which people struggle with self-acceptance and provide tools to assist in overcoming burdensome societal expectations.

A quick internet search of the term "societal expectations" yields mostly articles about how females are plagued by unrealistic expectations about body image. Unrealistic societal expectations are certainly not limited to the realm of the aesthetic, nor are they experienced only by females. Society appears to have opinions about motherhood, job performance, children's behaviors, relationships, masculinity and the list goes on and on. We can then turn to a debate of the origin of these "pie in the sky" expectations. Next, we have to factor in cultural considerations and geographic differences. Very quickly, a simple Google search to determine what impact societal expectations have on an individual's self-esteem expands to a complex topic! The negative impact of unrealistic expectations and the sources from which they are generated is by no means a new topic. The subject matter changes from year to year and blame has been placed on everything from the billboard

advertiser to the music video producer, but ultimately, the road to

self-acceptance begins with you.

Chapter 3

Self-Acceptance and Body Image

Self-esteem is not the only victim of unrealistic standards. Studies have shown that eating disorders, such as anorexia and bulimia, are associated with societal expectations about what is physically attractive. Discussions about this issue have been occurring for decades, yet photo shopping continues and trends like "thigh gaps" emerge. Models who have "thigh gaps" literally have a gap – a space – between their thighs and with the new trend, you can find them on Facebook, YouTube and the television. Suddenly, articles appeared all over the internet describing how to achieve this sought-after look. Here's the thing about "thigh-gaps" though – you can do absolutely nothing to achieve them! You either have them or you don't because your bone structure dictates it. Wider set hips allow for a thigh gap while more narrow set hips do not. So, no amount of dieting or exercise is going to achieve this ideal body. In 2014, major U.S. retailer, Target, controversially printed (extremely poorly) photo-shopped images of bikini-cladded models with "thigh-gaps". Time Magazine touted the ad as creating an "unhealthy depiction of a human body" and the online ad quickly disappeared.[i]

The constant bombardment of images of the "ideal" woman in the media causes many women and young girls to be dissatisfied with their own, very normal, bodies.

Body image involves our perception, imagination, emotions, and physical sensations of and about our bodies. It's not static, but ever-changing; sensitive to changes in mood, environment, and physical experience. It is not based on fact. It is psychological in nature, and much more influenced by self-esteem than by actual physical attractiveness as judged by others. It is not inborn, but learned. This learning occurs in the family and among peers, but these only reinforce what is learned and expected culturally. (Lightstone, 1991).

Culturally, that image changes with the wind, it seems, although it is never going to be achievable by the average woman because it is not realistic! According to a 2015 article in Harper's Bazaar, the current image "du jour" is even more unattainable than before- "…D-cup breasts, tiny waists, sculpted abs, big butts and thigh gaps inches-wide— all in one." Exercise and diet are not the ways that famous (and not-so-famous) women are achieving this look, either. According to Dr. Stephen J. Greenberg, a top plastic surgeon and media personality, "[w]omen are asking for larger, but more natural-looking breasts as well as enhanced buttocks, rounder hips and slimmer thighs." Referencing the current craze for thigh-gaps and butts with the exposure of Kim Kardashian, Greenberg goes on to say that, "[u]sing liposuction to shrink certain areas and liposuction combined with fat transfers to enhance others is definitely the new trend." The success of another Kim Kardashian endorsed trend, the "waist trainer", in day of old referred to as a corset, is addressed by plastic surgeon Dr. David Hidalgo, who states: "It's unrealistic to expect that these devices can fundamentally change body shape. There are potentially damaging physiologic consequences, including restricted breathing from interference with normal movement of the diaphragm, pooling of blood in the legs which could encourage clots to form and interference with function of the gastrointestinal tract."

A quick peruse of the internet yields links to research, studies and statistics about the percentage of women dieting and wanting to lose weight. Every form of media is inundated with advertisements for the latest diet, exercise regime, supplement or shake! The value of the weight-loss industry is currently estimated at almost $60 billion dollars annually.[ii] Feelings of low self-worth are associated with health-compromising behaviors in adolescence, such as substance abuse, early sexual activity, eating disorders and suicidal ideation.[iii]

Issues about body image are not limited to women and girls, however, though they have been dealing with them for decades longer than men. Rather than remedying the issues that exist for women, it seems as though we have just added unrealistic expectations for men to the equation. The 2014 TODAY/AOL Body

Image survey[iv] concluded that men actually worry more about how they look than almost anything else, including their health, relationships or career. Fifty-three percent of men said that they feel insecure about their appearance at least once per week. Almost 50% of the men who were surveyed shared that they think about their physical appearance several times each day. Other statistics derived from survey results include:

- 63% feel like they are overweight

- 53% do not like to have their picture taken

- 41% are concerned that other people are judging them based on their looks

- 44% do not feel comfortable wearing swimwear

For decades, Barbie dolls have been connected to the fight against negative body image for women, due to her body dimensions, which would be impossible to achieve for any woman. If Barbie were human, she would be unable to hold her own head up or walk upright and would not have room in her torso for all of her vital organs. GI Joe poses the same stumbling block for men. A well-known study from the late 1990s found that in 1964, GI Joe's dimensions would allow for him to have a 32-inch waist and 12 inch biceps. In 1991, however, he had a 29-inch waist and 16 ½ inch biceps. While women's expectations about the "perfect" body tend to result in a perceived need to lose weight, men tend to focus a little less on weight loss and more on muscle development.

Dr. Phillippa Diedrichs from the University of West England conducted a study to learn more about men and their desires for an "ideal" body. The results were absolutely staggering. Twelve percent (12%) of the men would sacrifice a year of their life to have an ideal body. Fifteen (15%) would trade two to five years. Five percent (5%) stated that they would sacrifice 6 to years and another 5% indicates that they would give up more than ten full years of their life to have an ideal body.

Recently, Tyler Kingcade, Senior Editor and Reporter for The Huffington Post, wrote an article entitled, *I'm A Man with Body Image Issues and Now I Know I'm Not Alone,* telling his personal story of a lifetime of self-hatred. In a follow-up article, Kingcade shares responses from men who identified with his story. A man named David told of his fears:

I'm a 20-year-old man and have struggled with my weight my entire life. I can't remember a time when I wasn't fat. And even now I still avoid going swimming just so that I don't have to take off my shirt in front of my friends. If I do get sucked in to going swimming with them, I usually keep my shirt on and my friends first try to encourage me to take it off, but when I'm unwilling, they give up and are accepting of it. However, because of this piece, I now have the courage to start learning more about not body-shaming myself and not caring what others think of my body. So I just wanted to say thank you. I haven't seen an article about a man body-shaming himself, and I needed that at this point in my life.

According to Kingcade: "Contemporary masculinity does not permit a man to admit his physique is less than ideal. But if men could be more open about their own insecurities, without fear of violating the unspoken rules of masculinity, we'd do better at accepting our flaws in our bodies." [v]

Chapter 4

Self-Acceptance in Western Society

The number of individuals suffering from mental illness has increased dramatically over the last few decades. Even more troubling, the number of individuals who are disabled as a result of mental illness has increased at an alarming rate. Mental health diagnoses, like depression and anxiety are seen throughout the world. However, research over the past decade, with organizations such as the World Health Organization (WHO), has revealed an interesting phenomenon. For example, such studies have determined that depression rates often are the highest in countries that are more affluent, including most Western countries and the United States. In a study published in *BMC Medicine,* an international team from the World Health Organization's *World Mental Health Survey Initiative,* interviewed over 90,000 individuals from eighteen different countries and assessed their mental health based on diagnostic criteria for major depressive episode. As a result of the findings, the World Health Organization estimates that as many as 121 million people worldwide suffer from depression. It is considered the 4th leading cause of disability in the world. In the 10 countries who were considered the most affluent, an average of approximately 15% of the population had suffered from depression at least once during their life. In addition, the level of impairment as a result of the illness was much higher among these individuals. This is compared to a rate of approximately 11% for low to middle income countries. The highest rate, 21%, was found in France and the United States followed closely behind with a rate of 19.2%. Among the affluent countries, Japan, Germany, Italy and Israel had the lowest rates, ranging from 7% to 10%. By and large, the rates in lower income countries were much lower, with the exception of Brazil, which had a rate similar to the United States and France. Even more troubling is the fact that individuals in the United States appear to suffer onset of depression at a much younger age than other countries. The median age for onset in the U.S. was 22.7. China had the youngest age, at 18.8.

Why are we seeing this phenomenon among Western countries? Is the problem that our society focuses on achievement and materialism over other pursuits? Many mental health practitioners agree that there is a connection between pursuing wealth and success and experiencing depression and anxiety. Another cliché', "Its lonely at the top", seems to have some validity, according to the very wealthy and successful, who maintain that high achievement often comes with a high price of isolation and loneliness. Long work hours often lead to the demise of personal relationships and depression creeps in. The pressure and stress that accompanies success also increases the risk of suffering from depression. Individuals who are "climbing the ladder to the top" also seem to be in constant competition-either with the business competitor or their own view of themselves. Successful individuals seem to never be satisfied with the "status-quo" and once they reach one goal, they move on to the next one. Supervisors and managers are guilty of doing this to their own employees. For example, if a sales goal is met, then a new one is set, often much higher. This can ultimately lead to dissatisfaction and feelings of hopelessness, which are associated with mental health disorders.

A parallel school of thought exists and research is being conducted as to whether the demands of modern Western society have resulted in the earlier and earlier onset of and increase in rates of depression. Some professionals believe that the human genome is more suited for being a hunter-gatherer, rather than for modern culture. Others maintain that societal factors such as high stress, lack of genuine connections and support systems, lack of exercise and poor nutrition have resulted in higher rates. Still others espouse the view that materialism plays a major role in development of mental health disorders.

So how do you overcome the need to achieve more and to "keep up with the Joneses"? How do you accept that you are good enough, that what you own is good enough and that you do not have to rise to some arbitrarily set standard if you do not wish to do so? Most of us tend to equate acquiring something new with positive emotions. Have you ever heard or used the phrase "retail therapy"? When you feel depressed, do you want to go and buy something new to cheer yourself up? You are far from alone if this is the case. Researchers have studied this phenomenon to find out what occurs in our brains when we acquire new things. A study[vi] published in *Neuron*, discusses what happens in the brain when we *think* about buying new things. Researchers flashed an image of a product on the screen and if the participant liked the product, it was noted that the nucleus accumbens, the pleasure center of the brain, was activated, meaning that it was flooded with dopamine – a "feel good" hormone. The reaction appears to be the same for thinking about buying something as it is for actually buying something!

Psychologists are not exactly sure why this occurs, but an article in *Psychology Today*[vii], discusses a few theories. Many scholars believe that the impulse to buy new and better things is simply a part of human nature. This theory is tied to Darwin's theory of survival of the fittest and the need to compete for scarce resources. Another theory is that the need to acquire new things is an evolutionary adaptation that keeps humans in a state of alertness. Psychologist Mihalyi Csikszentmihalyi states that dissatisfaction keeps humans constantly looking for something better and thus, improves the chances of survival. The theory continues that if an individual becomes complacent, then others can take advantage of them.

Though it remains uncertain as to why individuals derive pleasure from gaining new things, researchers do agree that the happiness does not last very long. In contrast, being too materialistic can actually make you more prone to depression, personality disorders and other problems. A study[viii] from Tufts University clearly shows that people who are focused on gaining material possessions have lower levels of well-being and psychological health than those who believe that pursuing material gain is unimportant. Research shows that holding strong materialistic values also makes individuals more prone to physical ailments, narcissistic and antisocial behaviors.

Psychological Science published a paper discussing an experiment in which people were repeatedly exposed to images of luxury goods, to messages that referred to them as consumers and to a barrage of words associated with materialism. Almost immediately, they became more materialistic and experienced anxiety and depression. They also became more competitive, selfish, had a reduced sense of social responsibility and were less inclined to be involved in more demanding social activities. Though these reactions were temporary, researchers expressed worry about what would happen to individuals who are repeatedly exposed to the same stimuli through the media.

One way that you can try to overcome an unhealthy relationship with material things is to honestly assess your shopping habits – why you shop when you do, what you are feeling as you shop, why you feel the need to buy bigger and better things, etc. As you do this, you will get a better understanding of what triggers you and will be better able to avoid the traps and pitfalls. When spending money, focus on purchasing "experiences" rather than "stuff". Researchers have found that the good feelings associated with spending money on an experience last much longer and you have the added benefit of making life-long memories.

There is absolutely nothing wrong with wanting nice things or spending money. There is a problem when you associate making more money and buying more stuff with happiness. This association often leads to a vicious cycle of comparing yourself to others, worrying about what other people think about us and then needing to make more money and buy more stuff to meet the gap. There is no set formula to prevent yourself from becoming overly materialistic, but addressing the issues of comparing yourself to others and being concerned with what others think can help.

One of the greatest barriers to self-acceptance is worrying about what other people think of you. Constant worry and anxiety about how others perceive you keeps you from being who you want to be and keeps you from achieving the things you would like to achieve. Why do we spend so much time worrying about what others think of us? We do so because we are conditioned from the time we are born to believe that there are certain ways to do things, certain ways to behave, certain things that must be achieved, etc. Some of these things are direct taught, but most of it is learned indirectly, just through every day living. Individuals develop "mental models" of how they believe life should be based upon these past experiences. These mental models are most definitely influenced by the media and society. How do you rid yourself of this type of worry? The first step is to realize that these "mental models" are not reality – that they exist only in your mind. Another helpful tactic is to assess whether or not you are guilty of making judgments about others. Neither worrying about others judging you nor judging others serves a good purpose in life, so rid yourself of both. The time and energy spent on both can better be used elsewhere. Finally, you must realize that ultimately, you have absolutely no control over whether someone is going to pass judgment on you or what that judgment will be. If you cannot control it, let it go – release it so you can experience freedom. The only thing you can control, is how you react to the situation and how you let it affect you.

Controlling your reaction begins with giving both them and yourself a good, hard, honest look. Let's start with "them". Who are they? If you are feeling insecure walking through a crowded mall and believing that people are looking at you and judging you, then you first need to come to terms with the fact that you DO NOT KNOW THESE PEOPLE. What value do these individuals have in your life? You may never see them again. You may not even care for them if you met them. They are in your life for a fleeting moment, so why should you consume your precious energy with worrying about what they think! In fact, it is pretty arrogant to think that when you walk into a space, everyone suddenly becomes consumed with YOU! Even if a few people look your way and think something negative about you to themselves, who cares? You shouldn't. Know also, that there are people in that crowd who feel the same way that you do. They may be looking at you and wondering if you are thinking bad things about them. Thinking this way seems simpler than it really is, however, and that is why you must practice. Train your mind to release these false thoughts and replace them with something positive. Self-talk is vital. Remind yourself of the truth every single time these negative thoughts creep in and you WILL see change.

Now let's turn to a discussion of "you", the only person whom you CAN control. In addition to self-talk, which is designed to change the way you think about others, you need to change the way you think about yourself. One way that you can combat such feelings is to work on yourself – build your confidence, broaden your horizons, focus on doing the things that you have always wanted to accomplish in your life. When you spend time doing this, not only do you enhance your life, but you do not have time to worry about what others think!

If you still find yourself having difficulties controlling your emotions, practice a very simple technique. First, become aware of what you are feeling and then observe that feeling with your mind. Think about it and any affect it is having on you physically. Assess any other thoughts that you have about it. The theory is that if you are able to observe this feeling in that manner, then it is not a part of you and you can release it. This objective way of viewing your feelings and emotions is empowering and places you back in control.

Chapter 5

Self-Acceptance and Social Media

To improve self-esteem and learn to accept yourself, you may need to unplug. Much research has been done about the impact of social media on mental and behavioral health. According to S. Shyam Sundar, Professor of Communications and co-director of the Media Effects Research Laboratory at Penn State, "[t]he types of actions users take and the kinds of information they are adding to their Facebook walls and profiles are a reflection of their identities." According to Sundar, people who are already experiencing problems with self-esteem are much more concerned about what other people post about them and we can surmise, whether they receive positive reinforcement through "likes" and comments. They are more apt to continuously monitor Facebook and delete anything that is negative or perceived by them as negative. "The more you get connected to Facebook, the stronger you feel that the items you post - the pictures, for example - are part of your identity and the more likely you are going to view these as your virtual possessions," said Sundar. Sundar is not the only researcher who has drawn these same types of conclusions.

A study conducted by The University of Gothenburg in Sweden[ix] found that as Facebook interaction increased, self-esteem decreased. Women seemed to be more negatively affected and to feel unhappy and discontent with their lives. A study from the University of Georgia also connected Facebook usage to self-esteem and possibly narcissism. The study pointed out that much of the activity on social networking sites is very self-focused, initially leading researchers to believe that use of the sites might boost self-esteem in those who lacked confidence. Researchers have found, however, that the exact opposite may be true and that those with self-esteem issues become more negative and may even make themselves "less likable".[x]

Research conducted by Amanda Forest and advisor, Joanne Wood, at the University of Waterloo focused on how students feel about Facebook. People with lower self-esteem saw positively and as a way for them to connect to others when they otherwise might not. A very interesting part of their studies examined what students posted on Facebook and how others viewed the posts. Posts made by people with low self-esteem were rated as negative and the raters, who were strangers, formed the opinion that they liked these people less! Therefore, people with low self-esteem may feel more comfortable with interacting on social media, but in reality, they may be harming their relationships. "If you're talking to somebody in person and you say something, you might get some indication that they don't like it, that they're sick of hearing your negativity," Forest says. "But when people have a negative reaction to a post on Facebook, they seem to keep it to themselves." [xi]

How do you know if social media is harming you? If you feel anxious, stressed or depressed after using social media, that might be a clue that it is time to reassess whether it is a helpful activity for you. You might be addicted to social media if you feel worried when you don't have access to it or cannot check it as often as you would like. People report immediately checking their phones as soon as they wake or if they wake-up in the middle of the night. If your posts, tweets and texts are interrupting the time you spend with "real-life" interactions, then it may be time to refocus your attention on building these relationships. One of the most damaging possibilities is comparing yourselves to others based on what you see on their social media sites. Remember that their profiles and posts are just a "snapshot" of their life that they have "photo-shopped" (often literally) to paint themselves in the most positive light. If you find yourself becoming jealous of people or, worse yet, reveling in someone's misery posted for all the world to see, then social media is greatly harming you in more ways than self-acceptance. Finally, social media usage can give you a false sense of relationship, when you are actually isolating yourself. Don't confuse the two. If you find yourself feeling extreme loneliness when not using social media or you can't enjoy time by yourself then you may be doing this.

It is completely understandable that you would not want to give up social media completely, especially since so many of our friends and family members use it as well. Do, what steps can you take to safe-guard yourself against the risks? The first step is to be aware of the risks, which you now are. The second step, is a familiar one. Conduct a self-analysis. How much time do you spend on social media? How much interaction do you have with friends and family outside of social media? How frequently do you check social media updates? Do you find yourself overly engrossed in the details of other people's lives? Do you compare your life to theirs? Do you feel depressed or anxious after using social media? Assess your answers to these questions and react appropriately through limiting your exposure or seeking help, if needed.

Chapter 6

Self-Acceptance and Feelings of Inferiority

A good portion of the population struggles with the results of comparing themselves to others and trying to achieve "perfection" and from low self-esteem or self-confidence. Unfortunately, distorted body image and issues with social media are common problems, but they are not the only areas with which people struggle. Whatever the struggle may be, a common set of tools can be used to overcome negative self-image and false beliefs. An individual must refocus, unearth the falsities behind the expectations and move toward self-acceptance. The definition of self-acceptance is fairly simple - accepting who you truly are, with all your strengths and your imperfections. It's a simple enough concept, but it takes time, practice and patience.

Take for instance, Layla's story:

> *It was not until I was in my forties that I had an epiphany that I could not recall a single time in my life where I felt like I belonged – that I was good*

enough. What a sad way to live life. Looking back, I do not know when these feelings began. I just know that they have always existed. In Elementary School, these feelings manifested in fears of "not fitting in" and that no one liked me. I felt like an outsider in every way, from the clothes I wore to how I interacted with others. I did not just feel this way around my peers, but also around adults. These feelings were not limited to school either. I also felt this way at church, a place where I should have felt very safe and very accepted. By all accounts, I should have been a very happy child. I was a straight A student, my teachers adored me and I won contests and awards. In fifth grade, I was even crowned queen at the annual school beauty pageant. I should have been so happy but I recall spending so many sad, sad days. I remember sitting in my front yard, feeling so lost and just wanting to disappear. As I was working through my new epiphany, and believing that I was making progress, I was at an outdoor concert one evening *and needed to use the restroom. Walking through the crowd, I was suddenly overwhelmed by that all too familiar feeling that I should not be here and that everyone who looked my direction could see that I was inferior to them.*

Many of my battles with self – most of my battles with self – stem from issues with my body image. "Being fat" seems as if it has always been an issue for me. I can pinpoint the beginning of that battle to about seventh or eighth grade when I suddenly gained a lot of weight. My parents put me on a diet. I recall taking my lunch of tuna, lettuce and pineapple to lunch every day. I did lose the weight by my Freshman year in High School, but it has been a struggle ever since.

From where do such feelings of inferiority stem? Many professionals theorize that our acceptance of self is based on how accepted we felt by our parents. If our parents sent us negative messages about who we were and what we could accomplish, then those followed us as we began to develop our concept of self. For some, feelings of self-worth are directly connected to performance and achievement because a message that value is connected to behavior was transmitted by the individual's parents. Many times, parents do this inadvertently and do not see that they are focusing more on negative behaviors than on positives. The child then begins to identify themselves and their worth with the negative behaviors – their failures.

In some cases, the parent's efforts to curb negative behavior, or what they perceive to be negative behavior, goes much further than a lack of positive parenting. For example, an overcritical father may be so frustrated with a child's inability to do well in academics that the child internalizes beliefs that he is stupid. A mother's efforts to help an overweight child lose weight may result in the child developing issues with body image that follow her into adulthood. Of course, there are cases of child maltreatment in which physical, sexual or emotional abuse can result in negative consequences throughout the life of the survivor. Many mental health professionals hold that, at the very least, most individuals learn from their parents that they are only conditionally acceptable. Therefore, if you don't live up to whatever arbitrary standards you have created in your mind, you are a failure.

Most children, while they will not recognize the damage that is occurring to their psyche, will recognize that they do not like feeling unfairly punished, berated or hurt by their parents. Ironically, however, they end up perpetrating these same ills on themselves, as adults. You may have heard it said that as we age, we turn into our parents. This is very true in the way that we treat ourselves. We internalize negative childhood feelings of angst, powerlessness and worthlessness until our ability to properly love ourselves is compromised. Our vision of self can also be scarred by pivotal moments when we experienced something so life-altering that it follows us throughout our life. For some, this might be bullying. For others, it might be an embarrassing incident at school. A statement made by a peer or adult authority-figure that exposes a perceived flaw can do almost irreparable damage in some. We then, unknowingly, punish ourselves in a number of ways.

Some people will try to compensate for feeling unworthy by undertaking self-improvement projects. Bookshelves, magazine racks, television programming and the internet are overflowing with materials on self-improvement, a testament to the fact that members of our society feel like they are not good enough and need to always be trying harder and doing better. Others will avoid taking risks, out of fear of failure. Still others live in the past or in worry about the future, constantly reliving past failures or in anxiety over what trouble may lie ahead. Living like this is a survival mechanism for the individual, a protective wall, that insulates them from feeling out of control. If they always expect the worst, then when failure comes, it is no surprise and they can say, "I told you so!" What the individual does not realize if that they are being robbed of the joy of living in the present moment. Constantly staying busy is another way that some people try to cope with feelings of inadequacy. Keep busy! Do more. Achieve more. Set goals! Unfortunately, in an attempt to make themselves feel better, some begin to look for and focus on other people's faults. Biologically speaking, the more times these types of thoughts are processed, the more the neural pathways become ingrained. They become like a well-worn, familiar old pathway that we can take without much thought and practically blind-folded.

We have identified the problem and discussed possible reasons for lack of self-acceptance, but how does one overcome and learn to accept themselves wholly and lovingly? Experts do not agree on a specific methodology, but it is clear that we must have the correct tools and practice. Lessons can be learned from religions, spiritual practices, secular therapeutic practices and anecdotal evidence from those who have succeeded in learning to love and accept themselves.

Chapter 7

How to Achieve Self-Acceptance – Religion and Spiritualism

"What you are is what you have been. What you'll be is what you do now." - Buddha. Buddhism focuses a great deal on knowing, accepting and being kind to self and meditation is one way to transform the mind to accomplish this. Meditation practices and the Buddhist concept of mindfulness, though in existence for thousands of years, have seen an increase in popularity in recent years. Mindfulness means being present and aware of our thoughts, feelings, body and environment, in the present moment. It also involves acceptance of these thoughts and feelings without judging them as being wrong or right, negative or positive. When we are aware of and living in the present, we aren't resorting to the old familiar pathway that leads to past failures or fears of the future. Renowned 7th Century Zen Master Seng-tsan taught that true freedom is found in being "without anxiety about imperfection." Imperfections are a natural part of existence and once we recognize and acknowledge that, we are better able to accept our own imperfections. As we lovingly accept our own imperfections, we begin spending less time trying to change ourselves to conform to a perceived standard of perfection and more time living in the present.

In fact, the concepts of mindfulness and mindfulness meditation have become mainstream and integrated into psychological therapeutic practices. Jon Kabat- Zinn, a molecular biologist from New England, feeling that others would benefit from mindfulness techniques, but would be deterred from their practice because of Buddhist origins, removed spiritualism and the belief of enlightenment, and created the Mindfulness Based Stress Reduction (MBSR) program, which was launched at the University of Massachusetts Medical School in 1979. His definition of mindfulness is, "the awareness that arises through paying attention on purpose in the present moment, and non-judgmentally."

The Greater Good Science Center at the University of California, Berkeley, in an article on mindfulness, notes the physical, psychological, and social benefits associated with its practice. Physical benefits include:

- Increased immunity to fight off illnesses

- Changes to the brain in areas linked to learning, memory, emotion regulation and empathy
- Reduction in obesity due to "mindful eating"

Psychological benefits include:

- Increased positive emotions and a reduction in negative emotions and stress
- Effective treatment of depression
- Reductions in pregnancy-related anxiety, stress and depression
- Reductions in stress-levels of health care professionals
- Reduction in PTSD symptoms in veterans

Social benefits include:

- Increased feelings of compassion and altruism

- Enhanced relationships

- Enhanced parenting skills

- Reductions in behavior problems in schools and benefits for teachers, including reduction   in depression and increase in compassion and empathy
- Reduction in anger, hostility, and mood disturbances among

  prisoners

The only time banging your head against a brick wall feels good,

is when you stop. This is a good theory to apply on your journey to self-acceptance. If doing the same things, talking the same talk and believing the same untruths has led you to negativity and self-loathing, then it is time to try something different. Emily Roberts, a licensed professional counselor, blogged about some very practical tips for becoming more mindful, building awareness and responding in a healthy manner to unrealistic expectations. Roberts equates operating with unhealthy thoughts to being on "autopilot". If you are constantly waiting for the next bad thing to happen or remembering errors of the past, you cannot be mindful or appreciate the present. She goes on to state that you do not have to join a yoga class or start meditating to get some very good results. Adding just a few mindfulness practices to your life can result in measurable changes. Just the act of slowing down or pausing long enough to recognize what is happening in the present can help dissipate negative thoughts, resulting in an increase in self-confidence.

Roberts offers the following, simple techniques that can be added to anyone's day: (1) Noticing the sights, smells, taste, sounds and feelings associated with particular events, (2) Focusing on breathing during the experience, (3) Allowing thoughts to just wander in and out of your mind, without analyzing them, (4)

Avoiding anything that is distracting from the moment, and (5) Letting go of any negative thoughts about yourself, others or the experience.

A very interesting technique is to do a "body scan" several times each day, noticing any sensations in the body, especially muscle fatigue or tension. Whatever thoughts pass through the mind during this time are simply discarded for the moment. Eventually distractions will happen less and less and you may even find yourself trying different mindfulness practices. Practicing this skill will allow you to bring it forth when you require it, for example, when you are particularly anxious.

You can turn practically any every day activity into a mindfulness exercise. You can practice mindfulness while taking a walk. Focus on what you are experiencing in the moment – the temperature, what you feel on your skin, the sounds, the smells, the color of flowers, the color of the sky, the formation of the clouds. A mindfulness technique to practice when using music is to isolate one voice, or one instrument, or maybe just the bass line of the song and focus on that through the end. Notice how this makes you feel and if you feel any differently than you normally do when listening to the song. Did you learn anything new about the song or yourself? When eating a meal, take your time and notice the textures, the smell and your thoughts as you experience the food. If you want to add to your mindfulness experience or learn about other methods and tools, there are many guided meditation practices on the Internet.

Opponents of mainstream religions often believe that such religions are diametrically opposed to self-acceptance principles and promote self-hatred. They point to teachings about the dangers of desires. Audre Lorde states, "We have been raised to fear…our deepest cravings. And the fear of our deepest cravings keeps them suspect, keeps us docile and loyal and obedient, and leads us to settle for…many facets of our own oppression."

Religious believers must recognize that without love for self, they cannot achieve everything that religion intends. Certainly, poor self-image hinders us in so many ways. Humanity is a reflection of religion and its characteristics and because of that all human beings deserve respect, compassion and love. A healthy view of self also includes a recognition that because you are human, you are imperfect. Understanding your self-worth necessitates accepting the work done by those before you. Realizing that this salvation includes you as an individual, even with all of your short-comings,

paints a vivid picture of your value.

Chapter 8

How to Achieve Self-Acceptance – Secular Approaches

The secular community has offered many ways to free oneself from unrealistic expectations and the harm they cause. Selena C. Snow, Ph. D, a clinical psychologist, believes that the first step in ridding yourself of unrealistic expectations is to recognize them. Having unrealistic expectations is normal, virtually everyone has them, but it is not healthy. Dr. Snow states, "Unrealistic expectations are potentially damaging because they set us and others up for failure." When those expectations are not met, feelings about self-worth are diminished and the resulting negativity can be directed inwardly or at others. Ridding yourself of these expectations can be hindered because we have been programmed to believe that having them is simply a part of good goal-setting. How does one go about recognizing that they are being unrealistic in order to strive toward self-acceptance?

Do you believe that everyone has to like you or become very upset when someone does not? Do you spend a great deal of time believing that the world should be fair or that justice should prevail? Do you believe people should always treat others with kindness and goodness? These types of beliefs all require a level of control that we, as individuals, do not have and can be indicative of someone who carries unrealistic expectations. There is nothing wrong with any of these beliefs, in and of themselves, but your response when people fail to meet these expectations can be very unhealthy. If you expect everyone else to react exactly as you would in every situation, when they don't, you can feel devastated or attacked unjustly.

Some people will not even allow themselves to feel the full extent of their emotions when something negative (or perceived as negative) occurs. They feel that painful thoughts or pessimistic feelings are signs of weakness. Depression or anxiety are taboo and not allowed. All of these types of emotions should be disallowed. Without realizing it, individuals who believe and react this way are trying to keep themselves safe. By defending against these emotions, they are building a barrier against the pain. Negativity and pain, however, are a normal part of life. Bad things happen to good people. People will disappoint us and let us down. Not allowing yourself to feel and process these emotions is extremely unhealthy. Self-acceptance means that we do not internalize such feelings, but rather we recognize them and move forward. When an individual learns to face their fear of pain, or other negative emotions, they will find it very "freeing" and may even be able to let go of anger or grief that they have possessed for years. Internalizing feelings or behaviors and hiding them from everyone else is usually a life-long habit, but can be broken. Some of the consequences of directing our feelings inward are: withdrawing from social activities, unexplained physical symptoms, and feeling lonely, unloved or guilty. Internalization can manifest itself physically and emotionally through depression or anxiety, changes in normal behavior patterns and loss of concentration and focus.

Unrealistic expectations, like the ones just discussed, tend to make some people harsh and unforgiving, either to themselves, others or both. They become fearful of change and inflexible in their ideas and actions. Miranda Morris, Ph.D., states that these types of people operate in a way that is "heavy on the should" – meaning that they have very fixed ideas about how they should be treated by others. An example might be that a spouse should know how you are feeling about something without asking. Another example might be that your children should always be respectful and kind. She holds that their thoughts follow an "if/then" format. Morris gives an example of the following: "If my spouse loved me, then he would know how I am feeling." The unrealistic expectation, when not met, then leads to the faulty belief that one is not loved. This type of faulty reasoning stands in the way of being able to have what is often most wanted in life.

Some expectations can even seem perfectly realistic and not unreasonable at all, but in fact, they are unachievable due to other circumstances. A parent may want a child to be good at sports, not an unreasonable expectation-thousands and thousands of young people are involved in sporting activities each year. However, some people are just not athletic or don't have interests in sports. If such is this case with your child, then the reality is that the expectation is unrealistic. In this case, the expectation can lead to even more problems, especially if a child is made to feel inferior because they do not excel in sports.

Dr. Morris suggests using humor as a way to deal with unrealistic expectations and promote self-acceptance. She suggests keeping a journal to list your unrealistic expectations as you discover them. As you reflect on them, do so with humor, saying things like, "That's funny that I think that way." Keep it lighthearted and accepting, acknowledging that they are based in faulty reasoning.

Dr. Snow advocates a technique she calls the 'double-standard' technique. Using this technique, you imagine what you would say to a close friend who think the same way that you do about a certain situation. The majority of the time, you will be much more compassionate toward a friend (or even a stranger) than you are yourself. After you recognize the 'double-standard' with which you are operating, you practice saying something more realistic and compassionate to yourself when self-deprecating feelings arise.

Reflecting on the effects of your expectations is a technique promoted by them both. Simply put, you consider whether an expectation is helpful. Does it help you to become who you want to be or achieve what you would like to achieve? Does it positively affect something for which you care? Does it help to build positive relationships or tear them down. Dr. Snow shares they her clients, after using this technique, find out that their expectations do not accomplish their goals at all or that they, in fact, hinder them. They often find that they avoid participating in risky activities all together because they are afraid of failure. According to Dr. Morris, if you find this to be the case, you can start to "release" the unrealistic expectation a little at a time. The key, however, is to have something with which to replace the unhealthy belief.

Replacing the unhealthy belief with learning to act out of compassion is an excellent tool. You must learn to be patient, accepting and loving of yourself and others. Relationships are much healthier when built in this way. For example, if a child fails to do something you asked them to do, rather than yelling at them that they never do what you ask, you can gently remind them, ask them to please take care of it and even offer help if they need it. The goal is accomplished, the relationship is enriched and the child is more likely to remember their chore the next time. The same is true for dealing with yourself. Instead of using negative self-talk when you "fail", learn to look at this situation as an opportunity to learn and perhaps do something differently next time.

Lastly, Dr. Morris maintains that you must remain flexible, starting with being flexible with change. This includes being flexible when others do not meet your expectations and allowing yourself to change your mind, respond in a different way than you have before and to work on relinquishing your unhealthy beliefs and unrealistic expectations.

Elisha Goldstein, Ph.D. uses a few other techniques with her clients to help them "mindfully" boost their self-esteem. She works with her clients to teach how to look backward to the origin of their negative message about themselves and recognize that it may have been a coping mechanism at one time, but is no longer useful. This recognition will allow you to slowly let the belief go. Another of her suggestions is very difficult for those who suffer from the inability to accept themselves. She asks clients to make a list of the things they like about themselves, followed by noting what they are feeling as they write down the items. This technique can be enhanced by also writing down what your friends might say about you. If a client has a particularly difficult time in knowing what others might think, they may need to ask close friends and family members for assistance.

Lindsey, a life-long sufferer of poor self-esteem, recounts how a craft project at a church Ladies' Retreat, helped her accept and learn to love herself. "The theme for the retreat was Proverbs 25:11 which says 'A word fitly spoken is like apples of gold in a setting of silver.' As a craft project, we were given small golden gift boxes and small slips of paper and instructed to write something thoughtful or nice about every single person at the retreat. The slips of paper were then placed in a golden box for each lady to take home. I had always had problems with loving myself and was having some very bad times. I began to read those little slips of paper from time to time and learned what people thought of me! Eventually, I began to see some of the things that they saw in myself. A simple craft project changed my life!"

The experience recounted by Lindsey is very much like a therapeutic technique that can be used by anyone. You can make a list, a box, a jar, a computer file – anything – and fill it with nice thoughts about yourself. It can be things that have been said to you by others or things you admire in yourself. Read the items in the file every day and any other time you need a boost. As with other mindfulness practices that have been mentioned, it is especially helpful to notice your thoughts, feelings and any physical reactions as you read the items.

Stepping outside of your comfort zone to try something new is a wonderful way to learn more about yourself and build a positive view of yourself. It really does not matter what you do, as long as you enjoy it and are doing it without the previous constraints that you placed on yourself. You do not have to be "good at it". It does not have to be perfect. Do something that you have always wanted to do – be someone you have always wanted to be. The freedom that comes from unhindered self-expression can permeate other areas of your life and lead to the self-love you are seeking.

The list of ways to help you achieve self-acceptance could go on and on. There are no "right" answers when it comes to what to do – you have to figure out how you can best be good to yourself! But, you don't have to do it alone and really shouldn't. Surrounding yourself with a loving, caring support system can help you see your self-worth and help you along your journey. By the same token, if there are "toxic" people in your life who do not support you or are tearing you down with their messages about your worth, then you need to remove them.

Chapter 9

Conclusion – There is Hope

The principles outlined in the previous chapters can be applied to any area of your life where you need self-acceptance. The possibilities include, but are not limited to: overcoming perfectionism, self-acceptance in the workplace, self-acceptance in relationships, self-acceptance in recovery or overcoming the need to be in control. The journey to self-acceptance is not always easy and can take time, but there is great hope for success.

You may recall the account of the little golden box craft activity that inadvertently became a tool of self-acceptance for a struggling woman. That account proves that you don't necessarily need fancy tools or a psychotherapist to change your life. That being said there are many free tools, activities and worksheets that are available online that can assist you. Don't be afraid to try them or come up with your own. Something as simple as writing affirmations on small notes and posting them on your refrigerator can go a long way in helping you retrain your mind.

When you find your hope waning, it may be helpful to read and meditate upon poems or quotes about self-acceptance. Here are a few to get you started:

"You yourself, as much as anybody in the entire universe, deserve your love and affection"
— Gautama Buddha

"The worst loneliness is to not be comfortable with yourself."
— Mark Twain

"I don't know if I continue, even today, always liking myself. But what I learned to do many years ago was to forgive myself. It is very important for every human being to forgive herself or himself because if you live, you will make mistakes- it is inevitable. But once you do and you see the mistake, then you forgive yourself and say, 'Well, if I'd known better I'd have done better,' that's all. So you say to people who you think you may have injured, 'I'm sorry,' and then you say to yourself, 'I'm sorry.' If we all hold on to the mistake, we can't see our own glory in the mirror because we have the mistake between our faces and the mirror; we can't see what we're capable of being. You can ask forgiveness of others, but in the end the real forgiveness is in one's own self. I think that young men and women are so caught by the way they see themselves. Now mind you. When a larger society sees them as unattractive, as threats, as too black or too white or too poor or too fat or too thin or too sexual or too asexual, that's rough. But you can overcome that. The real difficulty is to overcome how you think about yourself. If we don't have that we never grow, we never learn, and sure as hell we should never teach."
— Maya Angelou

"Friendship with oneself is all important, because without it one cannot be friends with anyone else in the world."
— Eleanor Roosevelt

"Love yourself first and everything else falls into line. Your really have to love yourself to get anything done in this world."
— Lucille Ball

"It's not worth our while to let our imperfections disturb us always."
— Henry David Thoreau

"If you begin to understand what you are without trying to change it, then what you are undergoes a transformation."
— Jiddu Krishnamurti

Face your deficiencies and acknowledge them; but do not let them master you. Let them teach you patience, sweetness, insight.

-Helen Keller

Be who you are and say what you feel, because those who mind don't matter and those who matter don't mind.

-Dr. Seuss

And then finally, when someone says something so well, there is no need to search (or write) any further, so we end with a quote from English comic actor, filmmaker and composer Charlie Chaplin:

As I began to love myself I found that anguish and emotional suffering are only warning signs that I was living against my own truth. Today, I know, this is "AUTHENTICITY".

As I began to love myself I understood how much it can offend somebody if I try to force my desires on this person, even though I knew the time was not right and the person was not ready for it, and even though this person was me. Today I call it "RESPECT".

As I began to love myself I stopped craving for a different life, and I could see that everything that surrounded me was inviting me to grow. Today I call it "MATURITY".

As I began to love myself I understood that at any circumstance, I am in the right place at the right time, and everything happens at the exactly right moment. So I could be calm. Today I call it "SELF-CONFIDENCE".

As I began to love myself I quit stealing my own time, and I stopped designing huge projects for the future. Today, I only do what brings me joy and happiness, things I love to do and that make my heart cheer, and I do them in my own way and in my own rhythm. Today I call it "SIMPLICITY".

As I began to love myself I freed myself of anything that is no good for my health – food, people, things, situations, and everything that drew me down and away from myself. At first I called this attitude a healthy egoism. Today I know it is "LOVE OF ONESELF".

As I began to love myself I quit trying to always be right, and ever since I was wrong less of the time. Today I discovered that is "MODESTY".

As I began to love myself I refused to go on living in the past and worrying about the future. Now, I only live for the moment, where everything is happening. Today I live each day, day by day, and I call it "FULFILLMENT".

As I began to love myself I recognized that my mind can disturb me and it can make me sick. But as I connected it to my heart, my mind became a valuable ally. Today I call this connection "WISDOM OF THE HEART".

We no longer need to fear arguments, confrontations or any kind of problems with ourselves or others. Even stars collide, and out of

their crashing new worlds are born. Today I know "THAT IS LIFE"!"
— Charles Chaplin

i   Stampler, Laura. *Can You Spot Target's Incredibly Awkward Photoshop Fail?*. Time. Web. 25 October 2015.

ii   The U.S. Weight Loss Market: 2015 Status Report and Forecast, Published on January 2015 by Marketdata Enterprises, Inc. https://www.bharatbook.com/healthcare-market-research-reports-467678/healthcare-industry-healthcare-market-research-reports-healthcare-industry-analysis-healthcare-sector1.html

iii   American Psychological Association. Task force on the sexualization of girls. (2007). *Report of the APA Task Force on the Sexualization of Girls.* Washington, DC: American Psychological Association. Web. http://apa.org/pi/sexualization.html

iv   Dahl, Melissa. *Six-Pack Stress: Men worry more about their appearance than their jobs.* Today. Web. 25 October 2015.

v   Kingkade, Tyler. *I'm A Man With Body Image Issues , and Now I Know I'm Not Alone.* The Huffington Post. October 25 , 2015.

vi   Knutson, Brian, et al. *Neural Predictors of Purchases. Neuron.* Volume 53, Issue 1, (2007): Pages 147-156. Print.

vii   https://www.psychologytoday.com/blog/out-the-darkness/201203/the-madness-materialism

viii   Kasser, Tim. *The High Price of Materialism.* MIT Press. http://ase.tufts.edu/gdae/CS/Personal%20Well-Being.pdf. November 10, 2015.

ix   Denti, Leif, et al. *Sweden's Largest Facebook Study.* Gothenberg Research Institute. http://hdl.handle.net/2077/28893. October 27, 2015.

x   Gentile, Brittany, et al. *The effect of social networking websites on positive self-views: An experimental investigation. Computers in Human Behavior.* Volume 28, Issue 5, (September 2012): Pages 1929-1933. Print.

[xi] Association for Psychological Science. *Facebook Is Not Such A Good Thing for Those with Low Self Esteem.* Web. October 27, 2015. http://www.psychologicalscience.org/index.php/news/releases/facebook-is-not-such-a-good-thing-for-those-with-low-self-esteem-html

Printed in Great Britain
by Amazon